THE CHICK'S
GUIDE TO BEER

Seven Simple Rules for the Beer Novice

CHEERS ON YOUR CRAFT
BEER JOURNEY!
JEN

JEN PRICE

ISBN-13: 978-0692876077 (The Chick's Guide to Beer)
ISBN-10: 0692876073

thechicksguidetobeer.com

Edited by T. Chanté LaGon
Art direction and book design by Tara Brown Designs, LLC
Illustrations by Leo Ramos
Published by TCGTB Publishing, Atlanta, GA

First Edition

This book is dedicated to my Dad, the first person with whom I shared a beer; to my Mom for being totally okay with it; to my family and friends who have supported me; and to the community who believes in me.

Thank you.

WHAT'S INSIDE

INTRODUCTION

Hi. My name is Jen and I love beer. I've loved beer all of my life – that's no exaggeration. One of my fondest childhood memories is enjoying a cold one with my Dad. I was and always will be a Daddy's girl. In my early years, he drove an off-white Volkswagen Beetle, and if you remember those old 'Bugs,' you'll recall that they were noisy. His was no exception. It was so noisy, I could hear him when he turned onto our street (and our house was the fourth one down the street). Dad's old VW was my cue that he was on the way. When I heard him approaching, I'd race to the kitchen, have my Mom hand me a glass and an ice cold High Life from the fridge, and then I'd wait. His after-work ritual was pretty much the same every day: He'd put his briefcase on the floor next to the blue chair in the living room, come into the kitchen, tease and prod my Mom for a hug and kiss, and give me a stick of gum. He'd open and pour the beer I'd prepped for him and then came my favorite part: he'd let me have the first sip. It was just the foam, but what did I know? I loved it. Partly because it was something that only he and I shared and also because I really liked beer. They say beer is an acquired taste. I may have gotten a head start on most!

Most folks don't have the same love story when it comes to their relationship with beer. That can go for both guys and girls, but since our beer culture is largely populated by men, my focus is on the ladies who would like to expand their knowledge. Believe me, I've been there: I have the same deer-in-the-headlights reaction whenever I walk into a wine shop. It's immediately overwhelming. I've wandered into a foreign land where I don't speak the language and can't even string together enough words or phrases to formulate an intelligent sounding question. That uneasy feeling is what motivated me to write this manual. I hope it helps the beer novice feel more confident when selecting a high-quality beer.

With over 80 recognized styles, the world of beer is a very wide one. It can be daunting and intimidating to people who are new to the idea of drinking beer. It can make you want to quit before you even get started. Even those who are motivated to learn may not be sure of where to start. Hopefully "The Chick's Guide to Beer" will help.

The guide is organized into Seven Simple Rules. Therein lies the information necessary for cracking the beer code. Topics include history, the brewing process and beer lingo. Beer styles and tips on how to properly serve beer are next, followed by tasting technique (because there is such a thing). Ideas for how to pair beer with food wrap up the Seven Simple Rules. The journal at the end of the guide provides you with a place to log the beers you try along your beer journey.

Learning about beer is so exciting. I encourage you to be adventurous and open-minded, to try lots of beers, and most of all, to have fun!

RULE #1
Know Your History

BEER

is one of the

MOST WIDELY CONSUMED

beverages in the world and played a significant role in the rise of civilizations across the globe.

There's a lot to be said about how

BEER BECAME A GLOBAL PHENOMENON.

This rule hits on the high points, from its discovery in the Middle East to its explosive growth in Europe and how it made its way to the States.

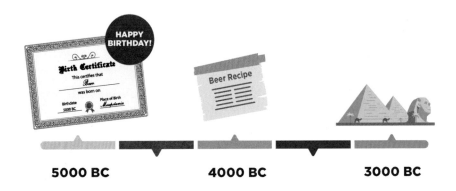

5000 BC   **4000 BC**   **3000 BC**

Some scholars date the birth of beer back to 10,000 BC, though the earliest known reference to a beer-like beverage dates back to ancient Mesopotamia (modern day Iran) around 5000 BC. The oldest written recipe ever discovered by archaeologists dates back to near 4000 BC and just happens to be a recipe for beer!

Let me give you a little frame of reference: In 4000 BC we don't really know what was going on because people weren't really even writing yet. That's how old and how important beer was to civilized cultures. In ancient times, lots of people drank beer instead of water. It is believed that in 4300 BC Babylonia, beer was more widely consumed and more pure than water. Prior to the invention of water purification systems, people actually used their water to brew beer, a much safer beverage to drink. In those days, the alcohol by volume in the beer was very low. So low that even children consumed it regularly.

The First Beer Chicks

Since beer was a basic household necessity, it was seen as a domestic chore and usually brewed by women. However, beer was also seen as a gift whose recipe was handed down to mortals from the gods. In ancient Sumerian culture, the goddess Ninkasi was worshipped as the head brewer to the gods. The "Hymn to Ninkasi" not only praised the goddess for her gift of beer but served as a recipe for how beer was made.

Beer continued to grow in popularity among ancient cultures. Historians believe that the Babylonians were the first to commercialize the brewing process.

The Original 'Super Food'

The Sumerians are credited with teaching the Egyptians how to brew and that's where the mass production of beer reached new heights with the construction of breweries. By 3000 BC, Egyptian breweries were very common and similar in size to modern day brewpubs.

Beer was a staple of the Egyptian diet and was considered a "super food" since it was packed with nutrients from grain. It played a uniquely significant role in the construction of the pyramids as workers were given rations of beer to sustain them throughout the day.

BEER IN EUROPE

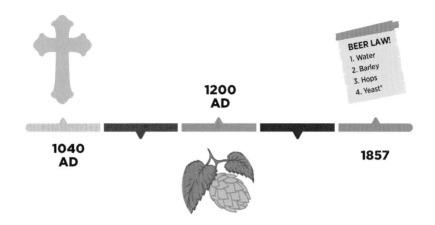

Fast-forward to 1040 AD when the first official brewery – the Weihenstephan Monastery – was established in Germany. That brewery is actually still around, making some of the world's best and most respected brews. Also around this time, hops are introduced as a main ingredient for beer in northern Germany.

By 1200 AD, the art of European brewing had rooted itself in Germany, Austria and England. Brewing became such a big deal that the Germans instituted a food purity law regulating and limiting the ingredients that could be included in beer. This law, called the *Reinheitsgebot*, was established in Bavaria in 1516 and stated that the only ingredients in beer could be water, barley and hops.

It took about 500 years for hopped beer to become a "thing" in England, but by the 1600s, nearly all English brewers used hops. In 1857, the *Reinheitsgebot* was amended to include yeast. This law has ensured that the fundamentals of beer, established hundreds of years ago, are basically the same today.

Not Just Known for Chocolate

The Belgians also played a major role in the proliferation of beer throughout Europe and the world, dating back to the Middle Ages (the 5th to 15th Century). Through conflicts and regime changes, they managed to hold on to their brewing traditions, undoubtedly borrowing some elements learned through multiple occupations. Belgian breweries were not beholden to the *Reinheitsgebot* and as such, often integrated a variety of spices and herbs like coriander, star anise and grains of paradise in beer recipes. This flexibility in brewing has resulted in so many Belgian beer, that experts say most do not fit into any particular style or category. They're simply Belgian.

BEER IN AMERICA

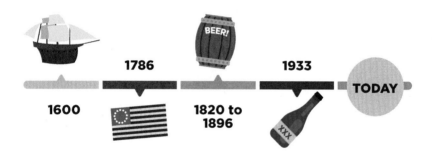

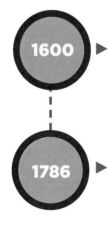

American brewing took off in 1587 with the first American beer brewed in Virginia using corn instead of barley. Legend has it that beer literally shaped our nation: The Pilgrims arrived at Plymouth Rock in 1620 because they were running low on rations (including beer) aboard the Mayflower. Brewing became a more common practice during the late 1800s. By 1786, both George Washington and Thomas Jefferson had their own private brew houses.

The Birth of the American Brewery

Commercial brewing in the United States took off in 1829 when D. G. Yuengling & Son, the oldest operating brewing company in America, was established in Pennsylvania. Yuengling, like Weihenstephan, also continues to produce beer. On the West Coast nearly 67 years later, Anchor Brewing Company opened and America found its first microbrewery.

Prohibition's Impact

Breweries and brewpubs continued to grow in popularity up until the time of Prohibition. The 1920 mandate shut down all breweries, wineries and distilleries. During Prohibition, bootlegging distilled spirits became prevalent. America's near 13-year dry spell ended when Prohibition was repealed in 1933. By that time the damage to the beer industry was done. Most breweries were unable to reopen and those that did began using more affordable but lower quality ingredients.

Beer's Big Comeback

Beer was slow to bounce back with the peoples' tastes leaning more toward distilled spirits. Still, beer production and consumption has steadily grown in America and beyond. Craft breweries continue to open up across the U.S. and homebrewing (made legal in 1979) accelerated a newfound interest in beer. Many American homebrewing hobbyists have enjoyed the craft and have become so proficient, they've gone on to open their own breweries.

Beer, Today

More and more breweries and brewpubs are opening every year. At the time of publishing, there were more than 3,400 known breweries in the U.S. and close to 10,000 worldwide. Still, beer remains highly regulated with each state having its own set of tailored regulations regarding the production and distribution of beer.

KNOW THE LAW

DESPITE ONGOING LEGAL BATTLES, BEER REMAINS THE THIRD MOST POPULAR DRINK IN THE WORLD. Here's how some of the laws vary from state to state.

- In Indiana, only liquor stores can sell cold beer. Don't even think about trying to buy beer, hot or cold, on Sundays in Indiana: All alcohol sales are prohibited.

- New Jersey lawmakers are considering the removal of a provision that requires breweries to provide a tour when selling their products for consumption onsite.

RULE #2
Understand What It Is
& How It's Made

THIS MAY BE A CRUSHING BLOW,

but those flavored malt beverages that you enjoy and call beer, like hard lemonades, pre-mixed cocktails or beer-margarita hybrids, are not beer.

Cider, which is made from fermented fruit and fruit juice, is not beer, either. On a basic level, understanding

WHAT BEER IS AND HOW IT'S MADE

is a great place to start.

WHAT'S IN BEER?

Beer is made from four very basic ingredients: water, grain, hops and yeast. Beer ingredients are very similar to those needed to make a loaf of bread. Trappist monks – who brewed beer at monasteries and sold it to the public to generate revenue – used to refer to it as "liquid bread" and relied upon it as their only source of sustenance during fasts. It's a pretty simple formula.

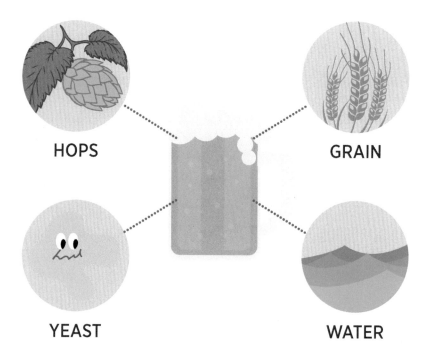

HOPS

GRAIN

YEAST

WATER

HOW IS BEER MADE?

Think about brewing beer like making a cup of tea: You take some herbs, spices, and dried tea leaves, combine that with hot water for a period of time, strain it, add honey or milk, and voilà! You have a cup of brewed tea. The beer brewing process, while not as simple, is very similar.

Malting

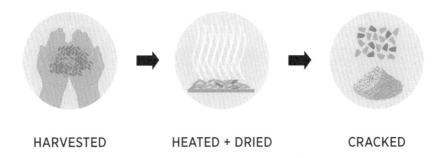

HARVESTED   HEATED + DRIED   CRACKED

The brewing process begins with selecting and preparing grain, the main ingredient (other than water) in beer, for brewing. The selected grain is then malted, a three-step process that includes steeping, followed by germination and finally drying of the grain. Barley is very often the grain of choice for malting, though sometimes other grains such as wheat or rye are used.

During steeping, raw grain is placed in large tanks where it is covered with hot water for up to 48 hours. During this time, the grain alternates between being fully submerged in water and being drained. Over a four day period, moisture is absorbed into the grain, activating the enzymes that kick off the sprouting process known as germination. Within four days, the sprouting process has begun and the grain is drained and transferred from the steep tanks to a germination compartment.

Storage in the humid germination compartment further encourages sprouting which in turn releases starch, a key ingredient for brewing. After about four days, the germination process produces the optimal amount of starch and the grain is removed for drying in an oven called a kiln for anywhere from two to four hours. The amount of time that the grains are dried in the kiln impacts the color and taste. Malted grain offers color, sweetness and body to beer. Grains that are dried for a short period of time are lighter in color and when used for brewing result in a beer that's lighter in color, body and flavor. Likewise, grains that are dried for a longer time become darker and contribute a darker, heavier bodied and more robust tasting beer.

Mashing

CRUSHED GRAIN   HOT WATER   1-HOUR

The malted grain is crushed and then combined with hot water for about an hour in a large vessel called a mash tun. During mashing, the grain and water are kept at an ideal temperature (anywhere between 145°F - 155°F) where the sugar that's contained within the grain is coaxed out. This is super important because sugar is eventually converted into alcohol later in the brewing process. The process of extracting the maximum amount of sugar usually takes about an hour. Afterward, the liquid is drained during a process called "lautering." This sugary liquid that remains is called "wort." The used or "spent" grain is discarded or sometimes sent to farms where it is used as feed for livestock.

Boiling

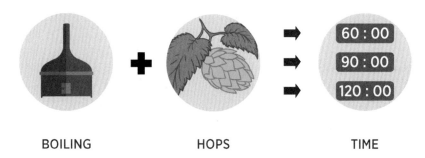

BOILING   HOPS   TIME

The wort is transferred to a brew kettle and is brought to a rolling boil for 60 to 120 minutes. During this time, any possible enzyme activity is halted, protecting the sugars that were released during mashing. The wort is also sanitized during the boil, killing any bacteria that may be present. A vigorous boil is also needed to get the most out of hops.

Hops are essential to the brewing process. They contain acids that, when boiled, release bitterness, thus helping to balance out all of the sugary sweetness of the wort. Hops are generally added during several stages of the boil – at the 60, 90, and 120 minute marks. The longer hops are boiled, the more bitterness they will impart. However, when hops are added during the last 10 minutes of the boil or less, they only have enough time to offer aromatic properties to the finished beer. Other spices and additives are also added during boiling to provide more flavor.

Fermentation

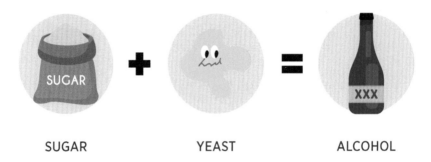

SUGAR   YEAST   ALCOHOL

At this point, all you have is hoppy wort. Fermentation is when the magic happens and the star of the show is yeast. No matter what type of beer is being brewed, the yeast does the same thing: It converts the sugar in the wort into alcohol.

After boiling, the wort is immediately cooled and strained to remove the spent hops, spices, and any additional particles. Once it's appropriately cooled, yeast is added or "pitched" and the process of fermentation begins. The liquid is allowed to ferment up to a few weeks depending on the style of beer being prepared. If the beer that's being brewed is meant to be an ale, it will ferment at a warmer temperature (between 60°F - 78°F) for a few days and in this case, ale yeast is added to the wort. If the beer that's being brewed is meant to be a lager, it is allowed to ferment at a much colder temperature (between 45°F - 55°F) for a longer period of time. A lager yeast that functions at much cooler temperatures is added to the wort. In either case, the yeast works until all of the sugar has been metabolized and turned into alcohol.

Hops can be added at the end of fermentation, however, at this point they do not impact the bitterness, they simply add aroma. This process is called "dry hopping."

Conditioning & Packaging

BOTTLING +
CONDITIONING

SHIPPING

ENJOY!

Once the yeast has completed its very important job of turning sugar into alcohol, the beer is allowed to mature or "condition." During this time, the yeast switches gears and starts its second job: creating bubbles, or carbonation. When brewers rely upon the yeast and sugar reaction to create carbonation, this method is referred to as natural carbonation. However, much of the carbonation created this way eventually escapes. Most brewers use the forced carbonation method, which pumps carbon dioxide into the product.

During conditioning, particles not removed during the brewing process are allowed to settle and may be filtered. The beer is also allowed to age between four to six weeks. Some styles can age for months. Aging the beer allows the flavors to further develop, creating a more complex and mellow beer. After the aging process, the beer is ready to be bottled, shipped and enjoyed!

DARE TO BREW A BATCH

WANT TO REALLY UNDERSTAND THE BREWING PROCESS? Try brewing your own batch at home! Online vendors and homebrew supply shops offer a variety of DIY kits, including 'clones' of some of your favorite brews. Many professional brewers kicked off their careers by brewing at home. Who knows...this could be your big break!

RULE #3

Talk the Talk

One of the most **CONFUSING** things about jumping into the world of beer drinking **MIGHT JUST BE THE LINGO.**

While this isn't a full dictionary, understanding **A FEW COMMON BEER BUZZ WORDS** will go a long way!

BEER LINGO

Alcohol by Volume [ABV] – a measure of the amount of alcohol in beer. Beer ABVs generally range from 4.5% to 14%.

Ale – beer fermented at warmer temperatures and with a specific strain of yeast that floats on top during fermentation.

Body – the weight and consistency of a beer when in the mouth. Grains used in the brewing process contribute greatly to the body.

Bottle Conditioning – a small amount of yeast and sugar may be added to brewed beer right before it is bottled and conditioned. This generally amps up the ABV and provides a bit more complexity.

Brewpub – a combination restaurant and brewery that creates and sells its own beer to customers. By the U.S. Brewers Association standards, a brewpub sells at least 25% of its beer on site in the restaurant and bar. In some states, brewpubs are allowed to bottle and sell the beer they produce on site to go.

Cellaring – the process of storing beer at a controlled temperature to allow it to age and further develop in flavor. Generally, beers with an ABV higher than 7% are ideal for cellaring.

Growler – a large glass container for getting draft beer to go. Think of a glass milk jug with a sealed top.

High Gravity – a brewing process whereby a stronger wort is produced and a beer with higher alcohol content results. High gravity beers generally exceed 8% ABV.

International Bitterness Units [IBUs] – the standard scale used to measure the bitterness of a beer. The scale ranges from 1 to 100 IBUs. Most human tongues cannot decipher anything beyond 100 IBUs.

Lager – beer fermented at cooler temperatures for a longer period of time and with a specific strain of yeast that sinks to the bottom during fermentation. Lagers tend to be more sweet and malty as compared to ales and can sometimes even taste like bread or dough.

Malts or Malted Grain – grain that has been properly treated and prepared for the brewing process. It is the primary ingredient in beer and contributes color, sweetness and body to beer.

Oktoberfest – founded in 1810, Oktoberfest was a celebration held on October 12th in Germany to celebrate the wedding of Prince Ludwig and Princess Therese of Bavaria. The celebration became an annual tradition and has continued year after year in Germany in Munich, the same geographic region as the wedding that bore the tradition. The official Oktoberfest event spans 16 days and is recognized as the largest funfair in the world. In 2015, an estimated 6 million guests were in attendance. Though a German tradition, Oktoberfest is celebrated in countries throughout the world. Additionally, the Oktoberfest (or Märzen) style of beer was a lager brewed during the month of March (Märzen is German for March) to celebrate the royal wedding. It is considered a seasonal and is typically medium to full in body with pronounced malty notes and low hop bitterness.

Seasonal – a beer developed during or for a particular time of year. They can be of any style and are usually brewed with ingredients that evoke the flavors of a holiday or are reminiscent of a certain season. For example, a winter warmer or Christmas Ale is brewed for enjoyment during – you guessed it – the Christmas holiday season. They're usually a bit heavier in body and may be spiced with cinnamon, ginger or nutmeg. Perfect for sipping next to the fireplace. Summer seasonals may combine a base beer of light body with fruit or juice as in the case of a Shandy or Radler. Though brewed and available for a limited time, seasonals can be enjoyed any time of year. It's really about personal preference. Storage of seasonals varies depending on style.

Session Beer – a beer that is lower in ABV, usually below 5% thus permitting the enjoyment of several beers in a "session" while still drinking responsibly. Though session beers are lower in alcohol, they still may be full in flavor.

WHAT IS 'CRAFT BEER'?

So, what exactly is craft beer? I'm so happy you asked! The Brewers Association defines American craft brewers as those that are **small, independent and traditional.**

SMALL

By **"small"** we're talking about breweries that produce 6 million barrels of beer or less per year. That accounts for about 3% of U.S. annual beer sales. And while 6 million sounds like a whole lot, it's really not. Some of the very well-known, large American breweries produce more than 100 million barrels annually. Most craft breweries produce far less than 6 million barrels per year.

INDEPENDENT

In addition to small, craft brewers are also **independent,** meaning less than 25% of the craft brewery is owned or controlled by another company in the alcoholic beverage industry that does not, itself, meet the definition of a "craft brewer." In other words, if one of the mega-breweries owns more than a 25% share of a craft brewer, it's no longer considered a craft brewery.

TRADITIONAL

Lastly, craft brewers are known for being **traditional** in their brewing practices. Alcohol can be made from many things: sugar cane if we're talking about rum; rye if we're talking whiskey; potatoes if we're talking vodka. But if you're brewing craft beer it is imperative that the alcohol in that brew comes from traditional ingredients (grain, hops, and yeast).

BEER CHICK TIP!

BEFORE THERE WERE HOPS...

BEFORE HOPS BECAME COMMONPLACE IN BREWING, herbs were often used to add bitterness, aroma and flavor to beer. These herbs, which could range from a singular variety to a mixture, were known as "Gruit" and were phased out with the introduction of hops.

THE TRUTH ABOUT HOPS

Hops are the flowers of a cone-like plant used in the brewing process to add bitterness, flavor and aroma to beer. Hops also serve as a natural preservative and belong to the Cannabis (hemp) family. *Hoppy* is a term commonly used to describe a beer that has a signficant hop flavor and bitterness. Hop flavors and aromas generally fall into seven categories:

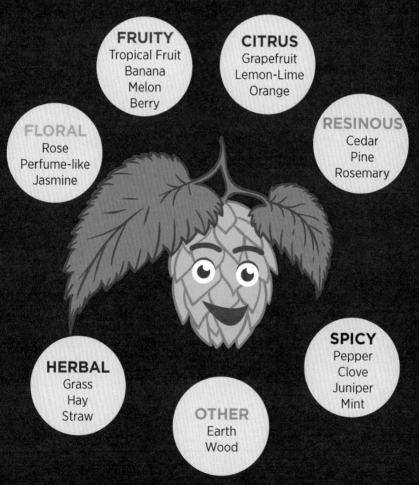

FRUITY
Tropical Fruit
Banana
Melon
Berry

CITRUS
Grapefruit
Lemon-Lime
Orange

FLORAL
Rose
Perfume-like
Jasmine

RESINOUS
Cedar
Pine
Rosemary

HERBAL
Grass
Hay
Straw

OTHER
Earth
Wood

SPICY
Pepper
Clove
Juniper
Mint

PICKING THE PERFECT BEER

for you is **JUST LIKE FINDING YOUR FAVORITE PAIR OF JEANS**

(and we all know how frustrating, yet rewarding that process can be).

You're going to have to test out a lot of styles to figure out what works for you and what doesn't,

but

WHEN YOU FIND THE PERFECT FIT,

you're going to jump for holy joy!

BEER CHICK TIP!

SMALL POURS + SAMPLES

VISIT A PUB WITH LOTS OF TAPS AND A FRIENDLY STAFF. Most places will let you pull up to the bar and try a fair number of small tastes before committing to a full pour. Beer folks are friendly folks and most craft breweries are proud of their handiwork.

MIX-N-MATCH

Most local grocery stores or bottle shops now allow you to mix and match from different styles to create your own custom six-pack instead of having to commit to an entire six-pack of the same beer. This is the perfect opportunity to try six different styles in one single shopping trip. Growler shops usually let you try just about anything they have in store, and if that's the case you should most definitely try it before you buy it!

FESTIVALS + TOURS

Other options for tasting a good number of beers all in one location include beer festivals and brewery tours. Beer festivals showcase a wide range of options from local and international breweries all in one place. Attendees buy a ticket or pay a cover charge and are free to taste as much as they want (responsibly). Check in with your local breweries for tasting room hours. Brewery visits are a great way to learn more about the brewing process and taste beers produced by a local brewer. At smaller breweries, you may be able to even meet and talk to the brewmaster.

BEER BUYING TIPS

So, what do you do when you're at the pub, growler shop or a bottle shop and you're faced with what seems like hundreds of options? How do you actually make a decision about what to try and buy? Start by thinking about four basic elements: **taste**, **feel**, **bitterness** and **finish**.

Taste – All of the ingredients used in brewing lend to the taste of the final product. It's probably one of the more prominent features in a beer, so establishing what you want from your beer in that category is the best place to start. Contrary to popular belief among beginners, all beer doesn't taste "beery." The taste can vary from spicy to fruity and tart, to coffee and cocoa-like. Determine what you want to taste first, and then move on to the next step, "Feel."

TASTE

Feel – Remember the definition for "body" in **Rule #3: Talk the Talk?** It refers to the feeling of the weight and consistency of a beer when in your mouth. That comes into play here. Decide if you want something that's light, medium or heavy in your mouth. This may be important if you prefer beers with a light feel during summer months and something a bit heavier during the winter.

Bitterness – You'll recall that hops are mostly responsible for the bitterness you experience in some beers. They're a necessary component in the brewing process, but can be well-balanced by the sweetness that comes from the grain. This is usually an easy determination to make: Do you want it hoppy or not?

Finish – After you've taken a swallow, what do you want the lasting impression to be? Some beers finish dry and clean like champagne while others end with a biting bitterness. Barrel aged beers and those with a higher ABV may finish with a boozy note. Whether you want a beer that lingers on the tongue or one that seemingly disappears, the finish can be a determining factor.

BEER CHICK TIP!

KEEP TRACK

YOU'LL EXPERIENCE A LOT OF DIFFERENT BEERS. Save the caps, growler tags and use the handy beer journal at the end of this guide to keep track of what you've tried. Be sure to note what you did and didn't like to help make purchasing decisions in the future.

PERFECT BREW LEGEND

THERE'S A BEER OUT THERE FOR EVERYONE!

Use this quick and dirty style profile chart to narrow down your options.

WHAT DO I WANT TO TASTE?

Super Light	**SL**	Spicy	**SP**
Malty	**M**	Fruity	**F**
Citrus	**C**	Tart	**T**
Chocolate	**CH**	Coffee	**CF**

HOW DO I WANT IT TO FEEL?

Light	**L**	Medium	**M**
Full	**FL**	Fizzy	**FZ**

DO I WANT ANY BITTERNESS?

No!	**N**	Maybe a Little	**M**
Yes, Please!	**Y**		

WHAT KIND OF FINISH DO I WANT?

Dry	**D**	Clean	**C**
Boozy	**B**	Lingering	**L**
Sweet	**S**		

	TASTE	FEEL	BITTERNESS	FINISH
PALE LAGER	SL M	L FZ	N	D
PALE ALE	SL F	L FZ	M	C
PORTER	CH CF	M	M	C
STOUT	CH CF	M	Y	S
INDIA PALE ALE	C	M	Y	L
WITBIER	SP F C	FZ	N	D
SAISON	M C	M FZ	M	D L
BELGIAN DUB, TRIP, QUAD	SP M	M FL FZ	M	B L
HEFEWEIZEN	SP F	M FZ	N	C
SOUR ALE	T	L	N	D

HEFEWEIZEN

TRIPEL

QUADRUPEL

WITBIER

PALE LAGER PALE

DUBBEL ALE

IPA

STOUT

PORTER

SOUR ALE

SAISON

COMMON BEER STYLES

Beer falls into two main categories: Ales and Lagers. But it doesn't stop there. Ales and Lagers can be further subdivided into 80+ beer styles. That's where it gets complicated! Here's a taste of 12 beer styles, each unique.

BEER STYLES

PALE LAGER

In Germany, this style is known as "Helles," which means "light." It is usually pale straw to golden in color with a very light body. This style comes across as more malty than hoppy, yet very light in flavor overall. The beer has a high amount of carbonation and finishes crisp and clean. It is one of the most popular styles in the world. There are European and American versions of this style. Pilsners are the Czech version of the pale lager.

ABV: 4.5% - 6%   **IBU:** 8 - 15

FAMOUS PALE LAGERS:
- California Lager (Anchor Brewing Co.)
- Mama's Little Yella Pils (Oskar Blues)
- Samuel Smith's Organically Produced Lager Beer (Samuel Smith Old Brewery)

SERVING TEMP: 38°F – 45° F

GLASSWARE:

PILSNER   STANGE   BEER MUG

COLOR RANGE:

BEER STYLES

PALE ALE

There are several versions of this beer, but across the board you can expect it to be golden to copper in color with a light to medium body. The original English version tends to be on the sweet and malty side. The American version leans toward a hoppy and sometimes mildly fruity profile. No matter the version, you can expect a dry and clean finish.

ABV: 4.5% - 6.5%   IBU: 30 - 45

FAMOUS PALE ALES:
- Grunion Pale Ale (Ballast Point Brewing Co.)
- Orval Trappist Ale (Brasserie d'Orval S.A.)
- 5 Barrel Pale Ale (Odell Brewing Co.)

SERVING TEMP: 40°F – 45° F

GLASSWARE:

NONIC PINT   **BEER MUG**

COLOR RANGE:

BEER STYLES

PORTER

Porters originated in England as a style made popular by the working class in the 1700s. The style was once very common and lost traction, but has been regaining popularity over the past decade. Because the grains are darkly roasted, porters range in color from dark brown to black and have a chocolate or smoky flavor. They have a medium body, lower carbonation and a dry finish.

ABV: 4% - 7%   **IBU:** 18 - 35

FAMOUS PORTERS:

- Russian River Porter (Russian River Brewing)
- Smuttynose Baltic Porter (Smuttynose Brewing Co.)
- Fuller's London Porter (Fuller, Smith & Turner Brewing)

SERVING TEMP: 45°F – 55° F

GLASSWARE:

TULIP

NONIC PINT

COLOR RANGE:

BEER STYLES

STOUT

A style of beer developed in Ireland that actually evolved from porters, stouts have a similar appearance and medium body. However, they usually have more pronounced roasted or burnt flavors. They will often taste of toast, coffee and chocolate. Stouts come in many varieties, including American, English, Irish, oatmeal and milk. Though nearly black in color, stouts are not heavy in nature and are traditionally lower in ABV.

ABV: 4% - 7%   **IBU:** 30 - 45

FAMOUS STOUTS
- Chocolate Stout (Rogue Ales)
- Guinness Extra Stout (Guinness, Ltd.)
- Cinnamon Roll'd Wake & Bake Oatmeal Stout (Terrapin Brewing Co.)

SERVING TEMP: 50°F – 55° F

GLASSWARE:

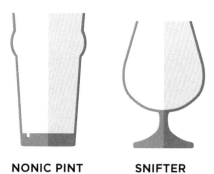

NONIC PINT   SNIFTER

COLOR RANGE:

BEER STYLES

INDIA PALE ALE

Also known as the IPA, this beer was made popular by the British and contains a significant amount of hops. The color is pale gold to deep copper and medium in body. IPAs are very hop forward in flavor and aroma. Since hops come in many varieties, IPAs can have notes that range from fruity, floral, citrus, earthy and pine. English IPAs are less hoppy compared to the American version.

ABV: 5% - 7%   **IBU:** 40 - 70

FAMOUS IPAS:
- Tropicália (Creature Comforts Brewing Co.)
- Two-Hearted Ale (Bell's Brewery)
- Sculpin IPA (Ballast Point Brewing Co.)

SERVING TEMP: 38°F – 45° F

GLASSWARE:

TULIP

NONIC PINT

COLOR RANGE:

BEER STYLES

WITBIER

This Belgian-style ale is made with wheat instead of barley and is typically pale straw in color. They are unfiltered beers which results in a cloudy appearance. Witbiers often taste and smell of warm spices like coriander and nutmeg and are brewed with orange peel which gives them a nice citrusy pop. Carbonation is high and hop bitterness is low. The American version is called a wheat beer.

ABV: 4% - 7%   **IBU:** 10 - 17

FAMOUS WITBIERS:
- Hitachino Nest White Ale (Kiuchi Brewery)
- Allagash White (Allagash Brewing Co.)
- Hoegaarden (Brouwerij van Hoegaarden)

SERVING TEMP: 40°F – 45° F

GLASSWARE:

WEIZEN GLASS   **TULIP**

COLOR RANGE:

BEER STYLES

SAISON

Also called "Farmhouse" beers, Saisons (French for season) were seasonal ales brewed and stored during the fall and winter and served during hot summer months to farm workers as a part of their daily ration during France's pre-industrial era. Today, this style is characterized by pale to light brown coloring, a hazy appearance and low hop aroma and bitterness. They vary in taste but are typically balanced between malty and citrusy tartness with some spice undertones. They have an effervescent and bubbly mouthfeel.

ABV: 5% - 8%   IBU: 20 - 40

FAMOUS SAISONS:
- Saison Dupont (Brasserie Dupont)
- Framboise Du Fermier (Side Project Brewing)
- Sofie (Goose Island Beer Co.)

SERVING TEMP: 45°F – 55° F

GLASSWARE:

TULIP

COLOR RANGE:

BEER STYLES

BELGIAN DUBBEL ALE

Characteristics vary widely for Belgian ales, but the Dubbel variety is deep amber to brown in appearance and may lean toward a sweeter, dark fruit taste (like fig, raisin or dried cherries) as compared to other Belgian Ales. Belgian candi sugar and yeast create high amounts of carbonation and a thick, frothy head when poured. One may detect very pronounced fruity and spicy aromas. The influence of hops is not readily noticeable.

ABV: 6.5% - 9%   **IBU:** 20 - 30

FAMOUS DUBBEL ALES:
- Trappist Westvleteren 8 (Westvleteren)
- St. Bernardus Prior 8 (St. Bernardus)
- Chimay Premiere Red (Chimay)

SERVING TEMP: 55°F – 58° F

GLASSWARE:

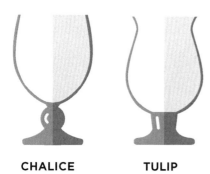

CHALICE   TULIP

COLOR RANGE:

BEER STYLES

BELGIAN TRIPEL ALE

Belgian Tripel Ales appear lighter in color than Dubbels and are highly impacted in aroma by the yeast used during the brewing process. Take a whiff and you may notice a fruity, banana scent, though not so much represented in the beer's flavor. Instead, Tripels taste mild and slightly spicy. Any presence of hops is masked by the spice and sugar, while alcohol content is high and more noticeable than with the Belgian Dubbel.

ABV: 7% - 10%   IBU: 20 - 30

FAMOUS TRIPEL ALES:
- La Fin Du Monde (Unibroue)
- Victory Golden Monkey (Victory Brewing Co.)
- Tripel Karmeliet (Brouwerij Bosteels)

SERVING TEMP: 45°F – 55° F

GLASSWARE:

SNIFTER   CHALICE   TULIP

COLOR RANGE:

BEER STYLES

BELGIAN QUADRUPEL ALE

While their names do not necessarily correlate to a mathematical relationship between the styles, it can be expected that a Belgian Quadrupel (AKA "Belgian Quad") will be stronger than the Dubbel and Tripel in every way. Hop bitterness is very low, allowing room for complexly layered flavors like caramel, fruit and spice to shine through. ABV reaches into the double-digits. When poured, Belgian Quadrupels display a thick, frothy head.

ABV: 9% - 13% +   **IBU:** 15 - 25

FAMOUS QUADRUPEL ALES:
- Trappistes Rochefort 10 (Rochefort)
- Trappist Westvleteren 12 (Westvleteren)
- Straffe Hendrik Heritage (Huisbrouwerij De Halve Maan)

SERVING TEMP: 55°F – 60° F

GLASSWARE:

SNIFTER   CHALICE   TULIP

COLOR RANGE:

BEER STYLES

HEFEWEIZEN

A German style ale brewed using wheat as the primary grain, Hefeweizens (AKA "Hefes") are a hazy, golden hue. The yeast creates an aroma reminiscent of clove and banana and the body ranges from medium to full. Hefes are known for being low in hop bitterness and may lean toward a malty, fruity flavor profile. They are often served with a lemon wedge (a debated tradition).

ABV: 4% - 7%   **IBU:** 8 - 15

FAMOUS HEFEWEIZENS:

- Weihenstephaner Hefeweissbier (Weihenstephan Monastery Brewery)
- Floridian Hefeweizen (Funky Buddha Brewery)
- Franziskaner Hefe-Weisse (Spaten)

SERVING TEMP: 40°F – 45° F

GLASSWARE:

WEIZEN GLASS

COLOR RANGE:

BEER STYLES

SOUR ALE

Also called Wild Ales because they were once fermented spontaneously by wild yeast (basically bacteria) floating around in the air, Sours are tart and sometimes have an acidic or even vinegar-like taste. They have no hop bitterness. An ancient style of fermentation, Sours have skyrocketed in popularity within the past five years. Lambic, Berliner Weisse and Gueuze are all part of the Sour Ale family.

ABV: 3% - 13%   **IBU:** 0 - 10

FAMOUS SOUR ALES:

- Red Angel (Wicked Weed Brewing)
- Oude Tart with Sour Cherries (The Bruery)
- Lips of Faith – La Terroir (New Belgium Brewing Co.)

SERVING TEMP: 40°F – 50° F

GLASSWARE:

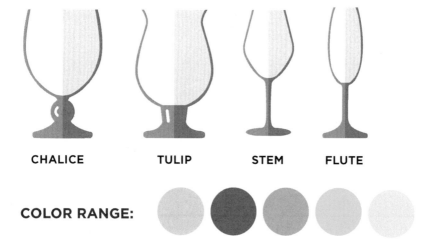

| CHALICE | TULIP | STEM | FLUTE |

COLOR RANGE:

BEER CHICK TIP!

UPGRADE YOUR STYLE

ARE YOU READY TO UPGRADE from your 'common' everyday beer to a higher quality, more sophisticated version? Start by identifying its style and then begin exploring craft beers in the same style 'family.' You'll be on your way to drinking a more posh brew in no time!

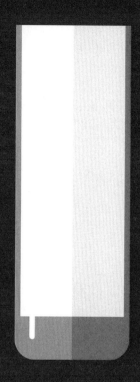

RULE #5

Do it Right

BEER DRINKING SHOULDN'T

necessarily be **FUSSY,** but if you're going to do something you may as well **DO IT RIGHT.**

That means paying attention to a few key elements: **SERVING TEMPERATURE, GLASSWARE** and the **POUR.**

TEMPERATURE

To get the very best out of the beer you're enjoying, it's important that it is served at the proper temperature. Beer that's too cold can shock the taste buds and prevent them from picking up on the more obscure notes. Drink a beer that's too warm for its style and you may never want to drink beer ever again. When enjoying a brew, you don't want it to be too cold or too warm...you want it just right. Goldilocks-style.

Simply put: There are optimal temperatures at which different beers should be served. Restaurants and pubs tend to serve most of their beer at one temperature, around 38°F - 40°F, which is super-duper cold. Much of that is to account for many factors. Beer travels sometimes hundreds of feet from the keg to the tap where it's poured and needs to remain cold during the journey. And if your favorite pub is a popular one, there's a high probability that your beer is going to sit for a spell before it's delivered to you. Storing beer at really cold temperatures ensures that, by the time your beer arrives at your table, it is still cold enough for you to properly enjoy.

SERVING TEMPERATURES

BEER STYLE	SUGGESTED SERVING TEMP
American Blonde Ale American Light Lager Belgian Tripel Ale Cream Ale European Pale Lager Kölsch Nitro Stout Pilsner	**VERY COLD** 38° - 45° F
Dark Lager Sour/Wild Ale	**COLD** 40° - 50° F
American Pale Ale American Porter American Stout Belgian Pale Ale Hefeweizen India Pale Ale Oatmeal Stout Saison/Farmhouse Ale Witbier	**COOL** 46° - 54° F
Belgian Dubbel Ale Belgian Strong Dark Ale Russian Imperial Stout	**CELLAR** 55° - 57° F
American Barley Wine Belgian Quadrupel Ale Scotch/Scottish Ale	**WARM** 58° - 61° F

BEER CHICK TIP!

CHECK THE TEMP

WHEN ENJOYING A BREW AT HOME, you have more control over the serving temperature. You should certainly take heed! A bottle thermometer is an ideal tool to add to your beer drinking kit. Wine bottle thermometers work just as well.

IT'S ALL IN THE GLASS

So, you've selected the perfect brew, it's properly chilled and you're ready to serve it up. But not any vessel will do. Always use a glass. Glassware makes your beer look beautiful, and since much of what we enjoy taste-wise is influenced by what we can see, the appearance of a poured beer can alter our perception of its taste, aroma and flavor. Believe it or not, proper glassware matters! A few more reasons why you should always use a glass:

- Beer glassware is meant to showcase and promote certain aspects of the beer and the design of glassware varies widely based on the beer style.
- A glass can help channel a beer's aroma to your nose, elevating your beer drinking experience.
- Glassware is often designed to showcase a brew's beautiful color and appearance.

In *Rule #4: Know Your Style,* you can find glassware recommendations for each style described.

But don't freeze your glassware. That's a no-no for many reasons. In the restaurant biz, it's not what they call "Beer Clean." Your freezer is home to lots of stuff, much of which you've forgotten about (like that turkey carcass from two Thanksgivings ago that you stored to make soup). When was the last time you cleaned it? Exactly. You know how sometimes your ice tastes like frostbitten broccoli? That's because your freezer is holding onto flavors, odors and lots of other tiny particles that will undoubtedly adhere to your glass and will taint how your poured beer tastes.

Then there's the issue of condensation. Once your chilled glass begins to come to room temperature, the frost begins to condense. That condensation (which is just water) pools and mixes with your yummy beer and boom, you've got watery beer. That's just gross.

So, the next time you're at a pub and they bring you a beer in a bottle or can, kindly ask if they can bring you an un-chilled glass. It's possible that the glass they bring to you will not be the proper glass for the beer style, but any glass is better than no glass at all!

In the handy dandy infographic on the following page, you'll find info on each of the glassware styles identified in *Rule #4: Know Your Style,* including why they're the ideal vessel for your brew of choice.

GLASSWARE MAINTENANCE

And now that you have all of this fancy glassware, you're going to want to take good care of it. Here are a few tips for how to treat your glassware right:

Hand-wash your glassware using mild detergent. Anything stronger will leave those ugly, murky streaks, which prevents light from getting through. Your beer won't look as cool. Heavy soap, when not properly rinsed, will undoubtedly impact the taste and aroma of your beer. The regular dish soap you use for all of your other dishes is just fine. Hand-washing will help prevent scratches, chips and streaking.

Allow glasses to air dry. Don't take a towel (even a clean one) and wipe them dry. That will leave lent and other debris on and in the glass and can even cause scratching. Using a drying rack or even placing the glasses mouth-side-down on a clean towel is a-okay.

Properly store your glassware. Mouth-side-up vs. mouth-side-down is an ongoing debate and really, there are pros and cons to both. Storing glassware mouth-side-down keeps dust and other particles from settling in the glass when it's not in use. However, storing delicately thin glassware in this manner increases the likelihood that the rim will be chipped. Using padded cabinet liners where you store your glassware can easily solve the potentially chipped rim issue right away.

GLASSWARE

NONIC PINT
ORIGIN: England
DESIGN: Tapered mouth, bumps make it easy to hold
PERFECT FOR: Pale Ale, Porter, Stout, IPA

BEER MUG
ORIGIN: Germany; Eastern Europe
DESIGN: Heavy and sturdy; high volume
PERFECT FOR: Pale Lager, Pale Ale

STANGE
ORIGIN: Germany
DESIGN: Narrow body and mouth help concentrate aromas of faint brews
PERFECT FOR: Kölsch, Pale Lager

PILSNER
ORIGIN: Bohemia
DESIGN: Showcases color & clarity; maintains proper head
PERFECT FOR: Pilsner, Pale Lager

TULIP
ORIGIN: Belgium
DESIGN: Flared opening promotes aroma & supports fluffy head
PERFECT FOR: IPA, all Belgian Styles, Porter, Witbier, Saison

WEIZEN
ORIGIN: Germany
DESIGN: Leaves room for large head; large opening & taper promote aroma
PERFECT FOR: Hefeweizen, Witbier

SNIFTER
ORIGIN: Borrowed from the Brandy & Cognac world
DESIGN: Inward taper leads aroma to nose; room for swirling
PERFECT FOR: High Gravity, Imperials, Belgian Styles, Barley Wine, Stout

CHALICE
ORIGIN: Plzen, Germany
DESIGN: Wide mouth promotes big sips
PERFECT FOR: Belgian Styles, Sour Ales

STEM FLUTE
ORIGIN: Germany
DESIGN: Shows off color, effervescence; keeps hands from warming beer
PERFECT FOR: Sour Ales, fruit beers

ALWAYS POUR

Much like with a red wine, pouring a beer allows it to open up. Even if it's into a coffee mug or a red cup, you want to always pour the beer from its original container (can, bottle, growler) into another drinking vessel. Think about how far your can or bottle of beer has traveled before getting to you. It has to go from its birthplace, onto a truck, and to a distribution warehouse. From there, it's put onto another truck and is then delivered to your favorite bottle shop where it sits until you come to pluck it. It's been lying dormant since it left the brewery, so when you get it home, you need to essentially wake it up. The best way to rouse a sleeping beer is to agitate it with a vigorous pour.

As shown in the infographic, you can ensure a proper pour in three easy steps. Most beers are poured as shown, however, some types (like stouts) are poured directly down the center of the glass. Pour it up and enjoy!

ENSURE A PERFECT POUR

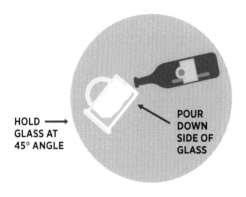

HOLD → GLASS AT 45° ANGLE

POUR DOWN SIDE OF GLASS

GRAB & POUR

Select the appropriate beer-clean glassware and hold it at a 45° angle. Begin pouring a steady stream of beer down the side of the glass.

STRAIGHTEN UP

After the glass is half full, straighten up the glass and continue to pour the beer at the same speed, straight down the middle of the glass.

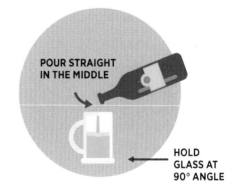

POUR STRAIGHT IN THE MIDDLE

HOLD GLASS AT 90° ANGLE

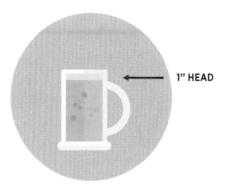

1" HEAD

FINISH

Continue pouring until the glass is full and there's a 1" layer of foam or "head." The beer can or bottle should be nearly if not totally empty.

HEAD, PLEASE

Let's talk a little more about that pour.

No matter what kind of beer you're pouring, you always want to leave some foam, also known as head. That's the good stuff (save the jokes, y'all)!

PERFECTION!

Remember, when a beer is brewed and left to ferment, the yeast has a chance to do its job, and that is to eat up all of the sugar in the wort. Carbon dioxide is a byproduct of this process, and when it is dissolved in beer, it creates carbonation. When CO_2 partners with protein structures that come from malted grain, they create foam or head. Yeast and hops play a part in foam creation, but to a lesser degree. When pouring a beer, a 1-inch head is the general rule of thumb, however, this varies by beer style as some beers (like Belgians and wheat beers) tend to be more carbonated and thus, produce more head.

Why is head important? Foam carries with it the aroma of the beer in addition to flavor. Since so much of what we think we taste when drinking and eating is actually coming from what we smell, having head on your beer means that both senses – taste and smell – are engaged at once. When taste and smell are in the same place, it's a party!

WHEN TO SEND IT BACK

FRESHNESS IS KEY! Here are a few things to look for to be sure you're not drinking a bad brew.

NO FIZZ: flat or dull beer may mean it's been on the shelf too long.

SNOWFLAKES: over time, proteins in beer will coagulate into sizeable flakes. It's pretty gross.

PAPERY TASTE: if it tastes papery or like cardboard, it's old or has been stored improperly.

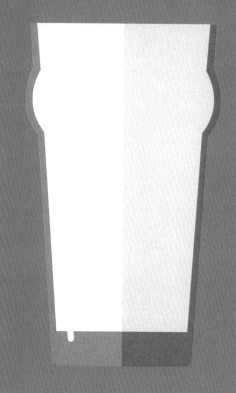

RULE #6

Always Swallow

SOME of the beer you drink **WILL APPEAL** to your palate right away. However, **NOT ALL** of the beer you drink will **TASTE GOOD** to you. That **DOES NOT MEAN** you should spit it out.

GOOD BEER DRINKERS ALWAYS SWALLOW.

PRESS THE RESET BUTTON

WHEN TASTING DIFFERENT STYLES, it's important to reset your palate. Sipping on room temperature water and snacking on unsalted pretzels in between samples will do the trick!

WHY SWALLOW?

Swallowing makes sense for a few reasons. Remember, smell and taste are closely related. Beer contains carbon dioxide gas which is released when you sip it. As you swallow, the gasses travel from your throat to your nasal passage, carrying some of the beer's flavor with it. To taste the full flavors the brewer intended, you must swallow.

Secondly, swallowing is the only way to learn and fully understand what you like (and don't like). Not all beer is created equal. Swallowing will give you the full picture, allowing you to pick apart the nuances of the beverage. Actually tasting beer is the only way you can begin to recognize and eliminate styles that don't appeal to you while you continue to taste and discover ones that you enjoy. Try to identify the more pleasurable aspects of beer and make a note of them.

Lastly, the notion of the tongue map – that certain parts of the tongue pick up on different tastes – is a myth. Scientists now know that the brain actually triggers and perceives taste at a much more significant level than the tongue. Taste buds do play a part, just not as big of a role in the beer drinking experience as once thought. However, allowing a beer to linger in your mouth and then swallowing it is highly encouraged. This practice allows you to notice the amount of carbonation or how the beer feels in your mouth. Most brews are complexly layered, so while you may dislike flavors found in the beer, perhaps you can appreciate the way the beer dances on your tongue or how quickly tastes evaporate afterward.

HOW TO PROPERLY TASTE BEER

SEE

Observe the color and look of the beer. Hold it up to a light to get a proper read on its appearance. What colors do you notice? How well can you see through the beer?

SWIRL & SMELL

Gently swirl your beer around in the glass to agitate it and stir up some foam. Stick your nose right up to the beer and take a deep whiff. What do you smell? Are you picking up on spices like clove and coriander? Do you smell citrus or vanilla undertones? Does it smell floral or perfume-like? What other scents are you reminded of? Be sure to take a few quick whiffs to assess the aroma.

SIP

When you take a sip, try to breathe in some air through your mouth in an almost slurping manner. Allowing the air to mix with your beer will further agitate it and ensure the flavors are at their most potent.

SWISH & SAVOR

Move the beer around in your mouth. How does it feel? Is it sweet and thick or thin and watery? A good beer will not have simply one flavor, but multiple tastes and sensations that will play out in your mouth.

SWALLOW

Beer must be swallowed to be fully appreciated. Swallow it slowly to pick up on all of the layers of flavor.

RULE #7

Try it with Food

YOUR BEER JOURNAL

Your Beer Journal will be a timeline and roadmap for your amazingly fun beer journey. Use the pages that follow to take notes on what you like and what you don't. Pretty soon you'll be teaching a friend to learn to love beer. Here's how you can get the best of it:

- Take note of when and where you are when trying new brews.

- Be sure to note the brewery and the beer's name, too. It will help when you're trying to locate it at your local bottle shop or pub.

- Recording the style will help keep track of what you like and don't. It makes knowing where to start much easier.

- Use the "Notes" section to document the aroma, flavor, mouthfeel, and other aspects of the beer that you notice.

- Finally, rate the beer. A failing brew is one you know to never try again!

YOUR BEER JOURNAL

DATE:

TIME:

LOCATION:

BREWERY NAME:

BEER NAME:

STYLE:

ABV:

IBU:

NOTES:

RATING: A B C D E F

YOUR BEER JOURNAL

DATE:

TIME:

LOCATION:

BREWERY NAME:

BEER NAME:

STYLE:

ABV:

IBU:

NOTES:

RATING: (A) (B) (C) (D) (E) (F)

YOUR BEER JOURNAL

DATE:

TIME:

LOCATION:

BREWERY NAME:

BEER NAME:

STYLE:

ABV:

IBU:

NOTES:

RATING: A B C D E F

YOUR BEER JOURNAL

DATE:

TIME:

LOCATION:

BREWERY NAME:

BEER NAME:

STYLE:

ABV:

IBU:

NOTES:

RATING: A B C D E F

YOUR BEER JOURNAL

DATE:

TIME:

LOCATION:

BREWERY NAME:

BEER NAME:

STYLE:

ABV:

IBU:

NOTES:

RATING: A B C D E F

YOUR BEER JOURNAL

DATE:

TIME:

LOCATION:

BREWERY NAME:

BEER NAME:

STYLE:

ABV:

IBU:

NOTES:

RATING: (A) (B) (C) (D) (E) (F)

YOUR BEER JOURNAL

DATE:

TIME:

LOCATION:

BREWERY NAME:

BEER NAME:

STYLE:

ABV:

IBU:

NOTES:

RATING: A   B   C   D   E   F

YOUR BEER JOURNAL

DATE:

TIME:

LOCATION:

BREWERY NAME:

BEER NAME:

STYLE:

ABV:

IBU:

NOTES:

RATING: (A) (B) (C) (D) (E) (F)

YOUR BEER JOURNAL

DATE:

TIME:

LOCATION:

BREWERY NAME:

BEER NAME:

STYLE:

ABV:

IBU:

NOTES:

RATING: A B C D E F

YOUR BEER JOURNAL

DATE:

TIME:

LOCATION:

BREWERY NAME:

BEER NAME:

STYLE:

ABV:

IBU:

NOTES:

RATING: A B C D E F

YOUR BEER JOURNAL

DATE:

TIME:

LOCATION:

BREWERY NAME:

BEER NAME:

STYLE:

ABV:

IBU:

NOTES:

RATING: A B C D E F

YOUR BEER JOURNAL

DATE:

TIME:

LOCATION:

BREWERY NAME:

BEER NAME:

STYLE:

ABV:

IBU:

NOTES:

RATING: A B C D E F

YOUR BEER
JOURNAL

DATE:

TIME:

LOCATION:

BREWERY NAME:

BEER NAME:

STYLE:

ABV:

IBU:

NOTES:

RATING: A B C D E F

YOUR BEER JOURNAL

DATE:

TIME:

LOCATION:

BREWERY NAME:

BEER NAME:

STYLE:

ABV:

IBU:

NOTES:

RATING: A B C D E F

YOUR BEER JOURNAL

DATE:

TIME:

LOCATION:

BREWERY NAME:

BEER NAME:

STYLE:

ABV:

IBU:

NOTES:

RATING:　A　B　C　D　E　F

YOUR BEER JOURNAL

DATE:

TIME:

LOCATION:

BREWERY NAME:

BEER NAME:

STYLE:

ABV:

IBU:

NOTES:

RATING: A B C D E F

YOUR BEER JOURNAL

DATE:

TIME:

LOCATION:

BREWERY NAME:

BEER NAME:

STYLE:

ABV:

IBU:

NOTES:

RATING: A B C D E F

YOUR BEER JOURNAL

DATE:

TIME:

LOCATION:

BREWERY NAME:

BEER NAME:

STYLE:

ABV:

IBU:

NOTES:

RATING: (A) (B) (C) (D) (E) (F)

YOUR BEER JOURNAL

DATE:

TIME:

LOCATION:

BREWERY NAME:

BEER NAME:

STYLE:

ABV:

IBU:

NOTES:

RATING: A B C D E F

YOUR BEER JOURNAL

DATE:

TIME:

LOCATION:

BREWERY NAME:

BEER NAME:

STYLE:

ABV:

IBU:

NOTES:

RATING: A B C D E F

YOUR BEER JOURNAL

DATE:

TIME:

LOCATION:

BREWERY NAME:

BEER NAME:

STYLE:

ABV:

IBU:

NOTES:

RATING: A B C D E F

YOUR BEER JOURNAL

DATE:

TIME:

LOCATION:

BREWERY NAME:

BEER NAME:

STYLE:

ABV:

IBU:

NOTES:

RATING: A B C D E F

YOUR BEER JOURNAL

DATE:

TIME:

LOCATION:

BREWERY NAME:

BEER NAME:

STYLE:

ABV:

IBU:

NOTES:

RATING: A B C D E F

YOUR BEER JOURNAL

DATE:

TIME:

LOCATION:

BREWERY NAME:

BEER NAME:

STYLE:

ABV:

IBU:

NOTES:

RATING: (A) (B) (C) (D) (E) (F)

YOUR BEER JOURNAL

DATE:

TIME:

LOCATION:

BREWERY NAME:

BEER NAME:

STYLE:

ABV:

IBU:

NOTES:

RATING: A B C D E F

YOUR BEER JOURNAL

DATE:

TIME:

LOCATION:

BREWERY NAME:

BEER NAME:

STYLE:

ABV:

IBU:

NOTES:

RATING: A B C D E F

YOUR BEER JOURNAL

DATE:

TIME:

LOCATION:

BREWERY NAME:

BEER NAME:

STYLE:

ABV:

IBU:

NOTES:

RATING: A B C D E F

YOUR BEER JOURNAL

DATE:

TIME:

LOCATION:

BREWERY NAME:

BEER NAME:

STYLE:

ABV:

IBU:

NOTES:

RATING: A B C D E F

YOUR BEER JOURNAL

DATE:

TIME:

LOCATION:

BREWERY NAME:

BEER NAME:

STYLE:

ABV:

IBU:

NOTES:

RATING: A B C D E F

YOUR BEER JOURNAL

DATE:

TIME:

LOCATION:

BREWERY NAME:

BEER NAME:

STYLE:

ABV:

IBU:

NOTES:

RATING: A B C D E F

YOUR BEER JOURNAL

DATE:

TIME:

LOCATION:

BREWERY NAME:

BEER NAME:

STYLE:

ABV:

IBU:

NOTES:

RATING: A B C D E F

YOUR BEER JOURNAL

DATE:

TIME:

LOCATION:

BREWERY NAME:

BEER NAME:

STYLE:

ABV:

IBU:

NOTES:

RATING: A B C D E F

YOUR BEER
JOURNAL

DATE:

TIME:

LOCATION:

BREWERY NAME:

BEER NAME:

STYLE:

ABV:

IBU:

NOTES:

RATING: A B C D E F

YOUR BEER JOURNAL

DATE:

TIME:

LOCATION:

BREWERY NAME:

BEER NAME:

STYLE:

ABV:

IBU:

NOTES:

RATING: A B C D E F

YOUR BEER JOURNAL

DATE:

TIME:

LOCATION:

BREWERY NAME:

BEER NAME:

STYLE:

ABV:

IBU:

NOTES:

RATING: A   B   C   D   E   F

YOUR BEER JOURNAL

DATE:

TIME:

LOCATION:

BREWERY NAME:

BEER NAME:

STYLE:

ABV:

IBU:

NOTES:

RATING: A B C D E F

YOUR BEER JOURNAL

DATE:

TIME:

LOCATION:

BREWERY NAME:

BEER NAME:

STYLE:

ABV:

IBU:

NOTES:

RATING: A   B   C   D   E   F

YOUR BEER JOURNAL

DATE:

TIME:

LOCATION:

BREWERY NAME:

BEER NAME:

STYLE:

ABV:

IBU:

NOTES:

RATING: A B C D E F

YOUR BEER JOURNAL

DATE:

TIME:

LOCATION:

BREWERY NAME:

BEER NAME:

STYLE:

ABV:

IBU:

NOTES:

RATING: A B C D E F

YOUR BEER JOURNAL

DATE:

TIME:

LOCATION:

BREWERY NAME:

BEER NAME:

STYLE:

ABV:

IBU:

NOTES:

RATING: A B C D E F

YOUR BEER JOURNAL

DATE:

TIME:

LOCATION:

BREWERY NAME:

BEER NAME:

STYLE:

ABV:

IBU:

NOTES:

RATING: A   B   C   D   E   F

YOUR BEER JOURNAL

DATE:

TIME:

LOCATION:

BREWERY NAME:

BEER NAME:

STYLE:

ABV:

IBU:

NOTES:

RATING: A B C D E F

YOUR BEER JOURNAL

DATE:

TIME:

LOCATION:

BREWERY NAME:

BEER NAME:

STYLE:

ABV:

IBU:

NOTES:

RATING: A B C D E F

YOUR BEER JOURNAL

DATE:

TIME:

LOCATION:

BREWERY NAME:

BEER NAME:

STYLE:

ABV:

IBU:

NOTES:

RATING: A B C D E F

YOUR BEER JOURNAL

DATE:

TIME:

LOCATION:

BREWERY NAME:

BEER NAME:

STYLE:

ABV:

IBU:

NOTES:

RATING: A B C D E F

BEER AND FOOD PAIRING GUIDE

Pale Lager	Pale Ale	Stout	India Pale Ale	Witbier	Saison	Belgian Quad
More Malty than Hoppy	Malt-Hop Balance	Coffee & Cocoa	Hop Bitterness	Crisp, Mild, Citrus	Fruit & Spice Notes	Caramel, Dried Fruit, Spice

IDEAL FOODS FOR PAIRING

Wings	Burgers	Steak	Blue Cheese	Salad	Quiche	Duck
Egg Rolls	French Fries	Stews	Coconut Curry	Seafood	Mussels	Brie
Pad Thai	Fried Shrimp	Dark Chocolate	Fettuccine Alfredo	French Fries	Brie	Apple Pie
Fish & Chips	Tacos	Lamb	Mac & Cheese			
	Grilled Veggies	Aged Cheese	Carrot Cake			

THANKS FOR HANGING OUT!

That wasn't so bad, was it? You're well on your way to discovering and learning more about beer. Remember – there will be some that you hate but also some that you love. That's the fun! Follow the steps in this guide and you'll shift from novice to know-it-all in no time! Cheers!

BEER and **FOOD** are best enjoyed **TOGETHER.** The colors, aromas, flavors and textures complement many kinds of food.

When **PAIRING** food with beer, begin by matching strength for strength: **LIGHT DISHES** go best with **LIGHTER BEERS** while **STRONG FOODS** work best with **ASSERTIVE BEERS.**

MATCH STRENGTH FOR STRENGTH

Pairing beer with food is actually much easier than many people think. When pairing food with beer, begin by matching strength for strength. It's a quick and easy way to rule out mismatched pairings. Think: Light dishes go best with lighter beers while robust foods work best with assertive beers. Matching strength for strength puts your beer and food on the same page, so to speak.

SEEK HARMONY OR BALANCE

Sometimes, you can find harmonies between beer and food. This is true when beer and food share complementary flavors and aromas. For example, desserts may pair well with a malty beer because they both share sweeter notes. Grilled steak and stout beer share roasted flavors and make a great and classic pairing.

Likewise, beer can be paired with foods that are in stark contrast with one another. In this scenario, the opposing flavors result in a better balance between the two. Spicy foods become more mellow when paired with malty beers, while hoppy beers balance overly sweet and fatty foods.

The graphic shows a few beer styles and how they pair with different food items.

RULE #4

Find Your Perfect Fit

THE INDIA PALE ALE

Hops are one of the most distinctive components found in beer. For those who favor a little hop bitterness, it's a welcome flavor. For the bitter averse, a hop-forward brew can be a complete turn off. As an ever present element in any beer, there are some that are more likeable to some palates than others. India Pale Ales or IPAs are the most common beers that showcase the hop in all its glory. IPAs were brewed in England during the Colonial Period. They have a debated history, but many believe that the hoppiness (along with the higher ABV) preserved the precious beer on its long voyage from England to India. Thus the name: India Pale Ale!

HOPPY = BITTER? NOT ALWAYS!

The bitterness that hops offer to beer is what gives the plant a bad name. Even though hops are a standard ingredient found in all beers, there are many styles that are pretty low in hop bitterness. Here are a few styles that you should look for:

- Hefeweizen
- Witbier
- Sour Ale

Even some India Pale Ales (which are known for being hop-forward beers) use hops that are more "juicy" in nature (think tropical fruit). Since they're IPAs, they're still BIG on hops, just not of the bitter variety.

BOLD FLAVOR + AROMA

Hops can be used at three points in the brewing process. How they impact a beer depends on when they're added:

- When hops are added during the **start** of the boil, they provide **bitterness**, which helps to balance out all of the sugar from the malted grain.
- When hops are added during the **middle** of the boil, they add a small amount of bitterness but mostly contribute **flavor**.
- When hops are added near the **end** of the boil, they add **aroma.**